Eggnog Cookbook for Holidays

Mark A Decent Celebration with The Most Popular Recipes

BY: Valeria Ray

License Notes

Copyright © 2019 Valeria Ray All Rights Reserved

All rights to the content of this book are reserved by the Author without exception unless permission is given stating otherwise.

The Author have no claims as to the authenticity of the content and the Reader bears all responsibility and risk when following the content. The Author is not liable for any reparations, damages, accidents, injuries or other incidents occurring from the Reader following all or part of this publication.

A Special Reward for Purchasing My Book!

Thank you, cherished reader, for purchasing my book and taking the time to read it. As a special reward for your decision, I would like to offer a gift of free and discounted books directly to your inbox. All you need to do is fill in the box below with your email address and name to start getting amazing offers in the comfort of your own home. You will never miss an offer because a reminder will be sent to you. Never miss a deal and get great deals without having to leave the house! Subscribe now and start saving!

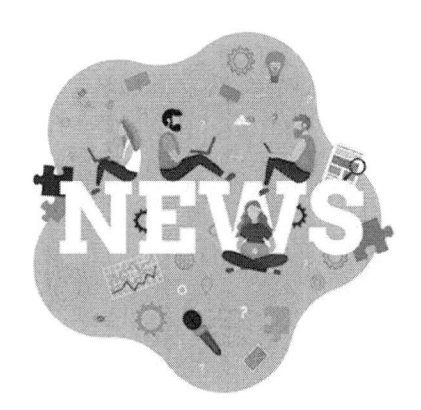

https://valeria-ray.gr8.com

Contents

Holiday Eggnog Recipes 8

Chapter I - Holiday Eggnog 9

    (1) Pumpkin Spice Eggnog 10

    (2) Banana Eggnog 13

    (3) Very Berry Eggnog 15

    (4) Cherry Eggnog 17

    (5) Pineapple Eggnog Punch 20

    (6) Eggnog Coffee 22

    (7) Peppermint Eggnog Shake 24

    (8) Eggnog-Lime Lassi 26

    (9) Peanut Butter Eggnog 28

    (10) Mocha Eggnog 31

Chapter II - Boozy Holiday Eggnog 33

(11) Hot Cider Eggnog with Brandy 34

(12) White Wine Eggnog 37

(13) Amaretto-Spiked Eggnog Latte 40

(14) Tropical Eggnog 43

(15) Black Christmas Eggnog 46

(16) Russian 'Nog 48

(17) Candy Cane Eggnog Martini 50

(18) Santa's Stout Eggnog 52

(19) Chai Brandy Eggnog 56

(20) Merry Eggnog Milkshake 58

(21) Champagne and White Chocolate Eggnog 60

(22) Irish Eggnog 62

(23) Christmas Creamy Eggnog 64

(24) Ice Cream Eggnog 66

(25) Holiday Eggnog 68

Chapter III - Eggnog Desserts Treats 70

(26) Fluffy Eggnog Fruit Dip 71

(27) White Chocolate Eggnog Truffles 73

(28) Baked Eggnog Cheesecake 77

(29) White Chocolate and Eggnog Streusel Cake 80

(30) Boozy Eggnog Crème Brulee 84

(31) Vanilla Eggnog Cookies 87

(32) Celebration Eggnog Trifle 90

(33) Pumpkin Eggnog Pie 93

(34) Cranberry and Eggnog Bread Pudding 95

(35) Holiday Eggnog Mousse 97

(36) Eggnog Flan 100

(37) Glazed Eggnog Donuts 103

(38) Eggnog and Cranberry Icebox Cake 106

(39) Gingerbread Eggnog French Toast Bake 109

(40) Festive Eggnog Fudge 114

About the Author.. 117

Author's Afterthoughts... 119

Holiday Eggnog Recipes

MMMMMMMMMMMMMMMMMMMMMMMMMM

Chapter I - Holiday Eggnog

MMMMMMMMMMMMMMMMMMMMMMMMMMMM

(1) Pumpkin Spice Eggnog

Pumpkin and the festive season go hand in hand, so what better way is there to celebrate National Eggnog Day on Christmas Eve than this pumpkin spice eggnog?

Yield: 4-6

Preparation Time: 15mins

List of Ingredients:

- 4 egg yolks
- ⅓ cup golden sugar
- 3 cups milk
- 1 cup 10% cream
- ½ cup pumpkin puree
- 1 teaspoon vanilla essence
- ½ teaspoons nutmeg
- 1 tablespoon pumpkin pie spice

MMMMMMMMMMMMMMMMMMMMMMMMMMMM

Methods:

1. In a mixing bowl, beat the egg yolks for 60 seconds.

2. A little at a time, add the sugar and continue beating until the sugar entirely dissolves and the yolks are pale.

3. In a pan, combine the milk with the cream, pumpkin puree, vanilla essence, nutmeg and pumpkin pie spice over moderate heat and while stirring bring the mixture to boil.

4. Remove the pan from the heat.

5. Gradually add the milk-spice mixture into the egg-sugar mixture while mixing vigorously with a whisk.

6. Return the combined mixture to the pan and cook until it registers 160 degrees F, for approximately 4-6 minutes.

7. Remove the pan from the heat and allow to completely cool.

8. Serve and enjoy.

(2) Banana Eggnog

If you are looking for the perfect drink to share for the holidays, then you can't go wrong with this banana eggnog recipe.

Yield: 2

Preparation Time: 4mins

List of Ingredients:

- 2 ripe bananas (peeled, chopped)
- 2 pasteurized eggs
- 2 tablespoons sugar
- 2 cups whole milk (cold)
- 4 tablespoons pure maple syrup

MMMMMMMMMMMMMMMMMMMMMMMMMMM

Methods:

1. In a blender, blend the banana along with the eggs and sugar until silky smooth.

2. Pour in the milk and add the maple syrup, beating until incorporated.

3. Pour the eggnog into the glasses and enjoy.

(3) Very Berry Eggnog

If time is short and you are expecting a crowd then this easy to make eggnog is the one for you.

Yield: 10

Preparation Time: 3mins

List of Ingredients:

- ½ gallon store-bought eggnog
- 1 cup milk
- ½ cup fresh blackberries
- 1 cup whipped cream

MMMMMMMMMMMMMMMMMMMMMMMMMMMM

Methods:

1. Combine the eggnog with the milk and berries, beating until frothy.

2. Serve in individual glasses and top with whipped cream.

(4) Cherry Eggnog

The flavors of eggnog and sweet maraschino cherries combine to create a festive treat to enjoy anytime.

Yield: 12

Preparation Time: 2hours 20mins

List of Ingredients:

- 1 (10 ounce) jar maraschino cherries
- 3 large eggs (slightly beaten)
- ½ cup granulated sugar
- ⅛ teaspoons salt
- 3 cups milk
- 1 teaspoon vanilla extract
- 1 cup half-and-half
- Fresh nutmeg (grated)

MMMMMMMMMMMMMMMMMMMMMMMMMMM

Methods:

1. First, drain the cherries. Reserve and set the juice aside.

2. In a pan, combine the eggs with the sugar and salt.

3. Stir in the milk and over moderate heat, cook while frequently stirring for between 10-15 minutes, until heated through.

4. Remove the pan from the heat.

5. Stir in the cherry juice reserved earlier along with the vanilla extract.

6. Cover and transfer to the fridge to chill, for a minimum of 2 hours.

7. Serve, garnished with nutmeg.

(5) Pineapple Eggnog Punch

If you are planning a big party, then you need a big bowl of pineapple eggnog punch.

Yield: 20-30

Preparation Time: 10mins

List of Ingredients:

- 2 quarts store-bought eggnog
- 2 (18 ounce) cans pineapple juice (chilled)
- 1-quart ginger ale (chilled)
- 2 cups mini marshmallows

MMMMMMMMMMMMMMMMMMMMMMMMMMMM

Methods:

1. In a punch bowl, combine the eggnog with the pineapple juice and ginger ales.

2. Scatter the mini marshmallows over the top and serve.

(6) Eggnog Coffee

Now you can have your coffee and enjoy a celebratory mug of eggnog.

Yield: 4

Preparation Time: 5mins

List of Ingredients:

- 1⅓ cups store-bought eggnog
- 2⅔ cups hot strong dark roast brewed coffee
- Whipped cream (to serve)
- Ground nutmeg (to serve)

MMMMMMMMMMMMMMMMMMMMMMMMMMMMM

Methods:

1. Pour the eggnog into a pan, and cook, while stirring until heated through. Do not allow to boil.

2. Stir in the brewed coffee.

3. Pour the eggnog into cups and serve garnished with whipped cream and ground nutmeg.

(7) Peppermint Eggnog Shake

Dessert and a drink in one! This minty eggnog shake will tick all those holiday flavor boxes.

Yield: 2

Preparation Time: 3mins

List of Ingredients:

- 1 cup mint ice cream
- ½ cup peppermint baking chips
- 1 cup store-bought eggnog
- ¼ teaspoons peppermint essence
- 1 candy cane (crushed)
- 1 candy cane (to stir)

MMMMMMMMMMMMMMMMMMMMMMMMMMMM

Methods:

1. In a blender, combine the ice cream with the baking chips, eggnog, and peppermint essence.

2. Process the mixture until smooth.

3. Pour the eggnog into a glass, and garnish with crushed candy canes.

4. Pop a candy cane in the glass to use as a stirrer.

(8) Eggnog-Lime Lassi

Eggnog gets zesty with freshly squeezed lime juice and is the perfect drink to wake up to on Christmas morning.

Yield: 1

Preparation Time: 4mins

List of Ingredients:

- 1 cup ice
- ½ cup store-bought eggnog (cold)
- 2 teaspoons freshly squeezed lime juice
- ¼ cup plain yogurt
- Pinch of salt
- Lime zest (grated, to serve)

MMMMMMMMMMMMMMMMMMMMMMMMMMMMM

Methods:

1. In a food blender, combine the ice with the eggnog, freshly squeezed lime juice, plain yogurt and a pinch of salt and puree until smooth.

2. Serve sprinkled with lime zest.

(9) Peanut Butter Eggnog

The quintessential festive beverage is creamy and smooth thanks to the addition of everyone's favorite; peanut butter.

Yield: 4

Preparation Time: 1hour 45mins

List of Ingredients:

- 4 eggs
- ¼ cup sugar + 1 tablespoon
- 3 cups whole milk
- ½ cup heavy cream
- ⅓ cup smooth peanut butter
- 2 teaspoons pumpkin pie spice

MMMMMMMMMMMMMMMMMMMMMMMMMMMM

Methods:

1. Divide the 4 eggs, placing the yolk in one bowl and the whites in another.

2. Using an electric whisk beat the eggs until pale. For approximately 2-3 minutes on low-moderate speed.

3. Add the ¼ cup of sugar, beating until the sugar is entirely dissolved in the egg mixture. Set the mixture to one side.

4. In a pan, combine the milk with the cream, peanut butter, and pumpkin pie spice.

5. Over moderate-low heat, bring to boil, while occasionally stirring to prevent the mixture from scorching.

6. Once it comes to a low boil, remove the pan from the heat and allow it to cool for 2-3 minutes.

7. Quickly combine the egg yolk mixture into the milk mixture. You will need to whisk immediately and fast to prevent the egg from scrambling.

8. Return the pan to moderate-low heat until it reaches a temperature of 160 degrees F. Remove from the heat. Transfer the mixture to a heatproof bowl. Place in the fridge to chill for 60 minutes.

9. Close to the end of the chilling period, and with a whisk attached to a stand mixer, beat the egg whites to form soft peaks. Add the remaining sugar.

10. Whisk the egg mixture into the chilled mixture, whisking until silky smooth.

11. Serve and enjoy.

(10) Mocha Eggnog

Enjoy a chocolate twist on classic eggnog so make up a batch to sip after caroling.

Yield: 6-8

Preparation Time: 10mins

List of Ingredients:

- 4 cups readymade eggnog
- 5 cups chocolate-flavored milk
- 1 cup heavy whipping cream
- 2 tablespoons granulated coffee
- 2½ teaspoons vanilla essence
- 1 teaspoon rum extract

MMMMMMMMMMMMMMMMMMMMMMMMMMM

Methods:

1. In a pan combine the eggnog, milk, ½ cup cream, and the instant coffee granules until hot through.

2. Take the pan off the heat; stir in the vanilla essence along with the rum extract.

3. In a bowl, beat the remaining cream until stiff. Dollop the cream over the eggnog and serve.

Chapter II - Boozy Holiday Eggnog

MMMMMMMMMMMMMMMMMMMMMMMMMMM

(11) Hot Cider Eggnog with Brandy

If you are looking for a festive boozy beverage this winter, look no further than this hot cider and brandy eggnog.

Yield: 4

Preparation Time: 25mins

List of Ingredients:

- ½ cup heavy cream
- 1 cup milk
- ½ cup cider
- 1 large egg
- ¼ cup sugar
- ⅛ teaspoons ground cinnamon
- Pinch ground nutmeg
- Pinch salt
- ¼ cup brandy
- Whipped cream (to garnish)
- Cinnamon sticks (to garnish)

MMMMMMMMMMMMMMMMMMMMMMMMMMMMM

Methods:

1. In a pan combine the heavy cream with the milk, cider, egg, sugar, cinnamon, nutmeg, and salt.

2. Cook over moderate-low heat for approximately 15 minutes, occasionally whisking until thickened.

3. Remove the pan from the heat and stir in the brandy.

4. Pour the eggnog into mugs and top with whipped cream and a cinnamon stick.

(12) White Wine Eggnog

It's quite common in Europe to use white wine when making eggnog so this year enjoy a White Christmas.

Yield: 20

Preparation Time: 25mins

List of Ingredients:

- 4 pasteurized egg whites
- ⅔ cup dry white wine
- ½ cup freshly squeezed lemon juice
- 1 tablespoon fresh lemon zest
- 1 cup honey
- 6 cups milk
- 1 quart half and half
- Nutmeg (freshly grated)

MMMMMMMMMMMMMMMMMMMMMMMMMMM

Methods:

1. Add the egg whites to a bowl and with a hand mixer beat until stiff. Set to one side.

2. In a pan, combine the white wine along with the freshly squeezed lemon juice, lemon zest, and honey over moderate heat, stirring until the mixture is warm.

3. Gradually add the milk along with the half and half while stirring.

4. Over moderate heat, stir until the mixture is frothy before removing it from the heat.

5. Fold in the stiffened egg whites.

6. Pour the eggnog into glasses and garnish with nutmeg.

7. Serve.

(13) Amaretto-Spiked Eggnog Latte

Caffeine addicts can have their coffee fix and join in the holiday spirit too.

Yield: 1

Preparation Time: 7mins

List of Ingredients:

- 1 cup eggnog
- 1 cup strongly brewed coffee (hot)
- ½ tablespoons sugar
- ⅛ teaspoons ground nutmeg
- ¼ teaspoons ground cinnamon
- 1-ounce amaretto liqueur
- Whipped cream (to garnish)
- Nutmeg (to garnish)

MMMMMMMMMMMMMMMMMMMMMMMMMMMM

Methods:

1. In a pan, heat the eggnog until very warm without allowing to boil.

2. Remove from the heat and using an immersion blender, froth.

3. In a bowl, combine the coffee with the sugar, nutmeg, and cinnamon, whisking together until combined.

4. Pour the amaretto liqueur to a large mug, add the coffee-spice mixture and stir to combine.

5. Pour the warm eggnog over the top.

6. Spoon the froth over the top and add a dollop of cream.

7. Garnish with nutmeg and enjoy.

(14) Tropical Eggnog

Coconut milk and spiced rum combine to create Caribbean-inspired nog.

Yield: 4-6

Preparation Time: 3hours 15mins

List of Ingredients:

- 2 (14 ounce) cans light coconut milk
- 6 pasteurized egg yolks
- ½ cup sugar
- 2 teaspoons pure vanilla essence
- 8 ounces spiced rum
- Ice
- ⅓ cup toasted coconut flakes (to garnish)

MMMMMMMMMMMMMMMMMMMMMMMMMMM

Methods:

1. Over moderate-high heat, in a pan bring the coconut milk to simmer.

2. In a bowl, whisk the egg yolks with the sugar and vanilla essence until light and smooth.

3. A little at a time, whisk half of the hot coconut milk into the egg-vanilla essence. Pour the mixture into the pan with the remaining coconut milk.

4. Over moderate heat, heat with stirring until the mixture coats the back of a wooden spoon, for approximately 2-3 minutes.

5. Strain the mixture through a fine-mesh sieve into a mixing bowl.

6. Stir in the rum, and transfer to the fridge for between 3-8 hours.

7. Pour the eggnog into a jug or pitchers, and serve, poured over ice.

8. Garnish with coconut flakes.

(15) Black Christmas Eggnog

This sambuca eggnog will get you in the party mood.

Yield: 1

Preparation Time: 2mins

List of Ingredients:

- 1½ ounces black sambuca
- 6 ounces eggnog

MMMMMMMMMMMMMMMMMMMMMMMMMMMMM

Methods:

1. In a glass, combine the sambuca with the eggnog.

2. Stir to combine and enjoy.

(16) Russian 'Nog

This nog is undoubtedly one of the best holiday drinks ever.

Yield: 1

Preparation Time: 3mins

List of Ingredients:

- 1 ounce vodka
- 1 ounce coffee liqueur
- 2 ounces eggnog
- Pinch of freshly ground nutmeg (to garnish)

MMMMMMMMMMMMMMMMMMMMMMMMMMMMM

Methods:

1. In an ice-filled old-fashioned glass, combine the vodka with the coffee liqueur.

2. Top with the eggnog and add a pinch of nutmeg.

3. Enjoy.

(17) Candy Cane Eggnog Martini

Nothing says festive season like a candy cane and this minty eggnog is sure to please.

Yield: 1

Preparation Time: 4hours 15mins

List of Ingredients:

- Honey (crushed, to rim)
- Candy cane (crushed, to rim)
- 1 shot vodka
- 3 shots eggnog
- ½ teaspoons mint essence

MMMMMMMMMMMMMMMMMMMMMMMMMMMM

Methods:

1. Add the honey to one shallow dish and the crushed candy cane to another.

2. Dip the rim of a martini glass first in the honey and second in the crushed candy cane, rimming the glass all the way around.

3. Combine the vodka with the eggnog and mint essence to a second glass, stir to combine.

4. Pour the eggnog into the rimmed martini glass while making sure you do not disturb the candy cane rimming.

5. Enjoy.

(18) Santa's Stout Eggnog

It won't matter if you have been naughty or nice if you leave Santa a glass of this stout eggnog! He is sure to come down your chimney!

Yield: 18

Preparation Time: 45mins

List of Ingredients:

- 6 large egg yolks + 2 large whites
- ¾ cup sugar (divided)
- Pinch of sea salt
- 12 ounces stout beer
- 1 cup heavy cream
- ½ cup dark rum
- Whipped cream (to serve)
- Chocolate shavings (to garnish)

MMMMMMMMMMMMMMMMMMMMMMMMMMMM

Methods:

1. Using a heat-safe bowl, whisk the egg yolks along with ½ cup of the sugar, until thickened and yellow. This will take approximately 2 minutes.

2. In a pan, bring the milk together with the salt to a gentle simmer. While constantly whisking, slowly pour the milk-salt mixture into the yolk-sugar mixture.

3. Return the combined mixture to the pan and over moderate heat, while constantly stirring; cook, for 3-5 minutes. The mixture should be thick enough to coat the back of a wooden spoon.

4. Strain the mixture through a fine nylon sieve into a bowl and remove and discard any solids before setting to cool, while occasionally stirring for 20 minutes.

5. Add the stout along with the cream and rum.

6. Cover and transfer to the fridge, overnight.

7. Whisk the remaining sugar together with the egg whites over a double boiler. Whisk until the sugar entirely dissolves and the mixture is warm and smooth, this will take between 2-3 minutes. (For eggs that are fully cooked, a thermometer inserted into the meringue needs to register 160 degrees F).

8. Remove from the heat.

9. Using a mixer set at high speed; beat the mixture until stiff peaks begin to form, approximately 5 minutes. Fold the mixture into the eggnog.

10. Transfer the eggnog to a punch bowl and top with a generous dollop of cream.

11. Garnish with chocolate shavings and serve.

(19) Chai Brandy Eggnog

Eggnog is sure to be a hit around the holidays, and there are many ways to make it, and brandy is a great option because it adds warmth as well as flavor.

Yield: 4

Preparation Time:

List of Ingredients:

- 2 cups store-bought eggnog
- 1 teaspoon vanilla essence
- ⅓ cup powdered Chai tea
- ⅓ cup brandy
- 1 tablespoon brown sugar
- 1½ teaspoons water
- 2 gingersnap cookies (crushed)

MMMMMMMMMMMMMMMMMMMMMMMMMMMM

Methods:

1. With an electric mixer, beat the eggnog with the vanilla essence, Chai tea powder and brandy.

2. In a shallow bowl, stir the brown sugar with 1½ teaspoons of water.

3. Add the crushed cookies to a second shallow bowl.

4. Coat the rims of the 4 glasses first with the brown sugar syrup and secondly in the crushed cookies.

5. Fill each of the 4 glasses with the eggnog.

(20) Merry Eggnog Milkshake

A merry milkshake for the Over-21s to rock your world!

Yield: 4

Preparation Time: 4mins

List of Ingredients:

- 6 cups vanilla ice cream
- 2 cups eggnog
- 2 ounces brandy
- 2 ounces dark rum
- 1 teaspoon ground cinnamon
- 1 teaspoon ground nutmeg
- Whipped cream (to serve)

MMMMMMMMMMMMMMMMMMMMMMMMMMMMM

Methods:

1. In a food blender, combine the vanilla ice cream, eggnog, brandy, dark rum, cinnamon, and nutmeg and blend until combined and silky smooth.

2. Top the milkshake with a dollop of whipped cream.

(21) Champagne and White Chocolate Eggnog

Classic eggnog gets a luxurious makeover with Champagne and white chocolate liqueur.

Yield: 2

Preparation Time: 5mins

List of Ingredients:

- 1 whole pasteurized egg
- 1¾ ounces cream
- 2 teaspoons Crème de Cacao Blanc
- 1 teaspoon maraschino liqueur
- 4 ounces Champagne
- Nutmeg (grated, to garnish)

MMMMMMMMMMMMMMMMMMMMMMMMMMMM

Methods:

1. Add the egg, cream, Crème de Cacao Blanc, and the maraschino liqueur to a cocktail shaker and shake.

2. Strain the eggnog into Champagne glass.

3. Fill the glass to the top with Champagne and garnish with nutmeg.

(22) Irish Eggnog

The Irish know a thing or two about having a good time and this boozy eggnog will undoubtedly get you in the party spirit!

Yield: 1

Preparation Time: 4mins

List of Ingredients:

- ¾ ounce Irish whiskey
- ¾ ounce Irish cream liqueur
- ¾ ounce hazelnut liqueur
- 1 ounce half-and-half
- 1 large pasteurized egg
- ¼ teaspoons ground cinnamon

MMMMMMMMMMMMMMMMMMMMMMMMMMMMM

Methods:

1. Add the Irish whiskey, cream liqueur, hazelnut liqueur along with the half and half, egg and cinnamon to a mixing pint and without adding ice, dry shake.

2. Add the ice to the mixer and shake it all about for an additional 20 seconds.

3. Strain the eggnog into a glass.

4. Garnish with cinnamon and enjoy.

(23) Christmas Creamy Eggnog

The earthy flavor of tequila works exceptionally well combined with eggnog and a splash of sherry.

Yield: 3-4

Preparation Time: 8hours

List of Ingredients:

- 2½ ounces sherry
- 2 ounces tequila
- 3 ounces sugar
- 2 whole eggs
- 6 ounces milk
- 4 ounces heavy cream
- Pinch nutmeg
- Pinch cinnamon
- Pinch salt
- Pinch pepper
- Nutmeg (to garnish)
- Star anise (to garnish)

MMMMMMMMMMMMMMMMMMMMMMMMMMMM

Methods:

1. Combine the sherry along with the tequila, sugar, eggs, milk, and heavy cream. Add a pinch of nutmeg, cinnamon, salt, and pepper, to taste.

2. Transfer to the fridge, overnight to chill.

3. Garnish with nutmeg and star anise.

(24) Ice Cream Eggnog

Your friends will be egg-static when you invite them round to share this thick and creamy adult-only eggnog.

Yield: 8-10

Preparation Time:

List of Ingredients:

- 10 scoops vanilla ice cream
- 1½ cups store-bought eggnog
- ½ cup bourbon
- ½ brandy
- 2-3 tablespoons orange liqueur
- ¼ teaspoons nutmeg (grated)
- Grated chocolate (to garnish)

MMMMMMMMMMMMMMMMMMMMMMMMMMMM

Methods:

1. In a food blender, combine the ice cream with the eggnog, bourbon, brandy, orange liqueur and nutmeg, and on the lowest speed, process until silky smooth.

2. Pour into glasses and garnish with grated chocolate.

(25) Holiday Eggnog

For a drink packed with holiday spirit opt for this eggnog recipe.

Yield: 1

Preparation Time: 3mins

List of Ingredients:

- 1 ounce gin
- ½ ounce cognac
- ¾ ounce simple syrup
- 3 ounces almond milk
- 1 ounce heavy cream
- 1 medium pasteurized egg
- Star anise (to garnish)

MMMMMMMMMMMMMMMMMMMMMMMMMMMM

Methods:

1. Add the gin, cognac, simple syrup, almond milk, heavy cream and the egg to an ice shaker and dry shake.

2. Add the ice and shake it all about until chilled.

3. Strain the eggnog into a rocks glass and garnish with star anise.

Chapter III - Eggnog Desserts Treats

MMMMMMMMMMMMMMMMMMMMMMMMMM

(26) Fluffy Eggnog Fruit Dip

A fluffy festive dip is perfect for movie nights and holiday get-together. Grab some fresh fruit and get dipping!

Yield: 18-20

Preparation Time: 3hours 5mins

List of Ingredients:

- 1 cup readymade eggnog
- 1 (3.4 ounce) box instant vanilla pudding mix
- Pinch ground nutmeg
- 8 ounces frozen whip topping (thawed)
- Fresh fruit (to serve)

MMMMMMMMMMMMMMMMMMMMMMMMMMMM

Methods:

1. Stir together the eggnog and pudding mix in a bowl until combined.

2. Fold in the nutmeg and whip topping until incorporated.

3. Chill for a few hours until thick.

4. Serve with fresh fruit.

(27) White Chocolate Eggnog Truffles

Make a batch of these tempting eggnog truffles and serve as an after-dinner treat for your next party or get-together.

Yield: 30

Preparation Time: 1hour 5mins

List of Ingredients:

- 1 cup white chocolate chips
- ½ cup store-bought eggnog
- 2 ¾ cups vanilla sandwich cookies (crushed, divided)
- 1 (24 ounce) pack vanilla almond bark

MMMMMMMMMMMMMMMMMMMMMMMMMMM

Methods:

1. In a microwave-safe bowl, heat the chocolate chips in 30-second increments for 60-90 seconds, stirring between increments.

2. When the chocolate is melted, stir in the eggnog add the crushed cookies and mix to combine.

3. Transfer the mixture to the freezer until thickened, for 15-20 minutes.

4. Using a tablespoon, scoop the dough to create evenly-sized truffles.

5. Roll each truffle between clean hands to make smooth truffles.

6. Arrange the truffles on a baking sheet lined with parchment paper and place in the freezer to harden, for 15 minutes.

7. Using a double boiler, melt the bark.

8. Remove the truffles from the freezer and dip each truffle in the melted almond bark.

9. Arrange the coated truffles on the parchment paper lined baking sheet, scatter the remaining cookie crumbs over the top and set aside to set.

10. Serve and enjoy.

(28) Baked Eggnog Cheesecake

This baked eggnog cheesecake is everything a good cheesecake should be; rich, creamy, and indulgent.

Yield: 16

Preparation Time: 9hours 30mins

List of Ingredients:

Base:

- 1 cup crumbled graham crackers
- 3 tablespoons melted butter
- 2 tablespoons granulated sugar

Cheesecake:

- 1½ pounds full-fat cream cheese (at room temperature)
- 3 tablespoons all-purpose flour
- 1 cup granulated sugar
- 2 eggs (beaten)
- ½ teaspoons rum essence
- ¾ cup readymade eggnog
- Pinch nutmeg

MMMMMMMMMMMMMMMMMMMMMMMMMMMM

Methods:

1. Preheat the main oven to 325 degrees F. Grease a 9" springform tin.

2. First, make the base. Combine the cracker crumbs, butter, and sugar. Press the mixture into the base of the tin and bake for 10 minutes. Allow to cool.

3. Next, prepare the topping. Beat together the cream cheese, flour, and sugar until combined. Beat in the eggs, followed by the rum essence, eggnog, and nutmeg. Pour the mixture on top of the crust.

4. Wrap a double layer of thick aluminum foil around the springform tin and arrange in a roasting tin. Pour in 1" of boiling water. Return to the oven and bake for just over 45 minutes until set. Allow to cool completely. Chill overnight.

(29) White Chocolate and Eggnog Streusel Cake

White chocolate and eggnog cake with a crumbly streusel topping and rum glaze is a next level sweet treat.

Yield: 8

Preparation Time: 1hour 10mins

List of Ingredients:

Cake:

- 1½ teaspoons baking powder
- 1½ cups all-purpose flour
- ½ teaspoons cinnamon
- ½ teaspoons salt
- ¼ teaspoons nutmeg
- 1 cup granulated sugar
- 6 tablespoons unsalted butter (softened)
- 1 egg
- ½ teaspoons rum essence
- 1 teaspoon of vanilla essence
- ½ cup ready-made eggnog

Streusel:

- ⅓ cup brown sugar
- ⅓ cup all-purpose flour
- ¼ teaspoons nutmeg
- ½ teaspoons cinnamon
- 4 tablespoons butter (chilled, chopped)
- ½ cup white choc chips

Glaze:

- 2 tablespoons ready-made eggnog
- ¾ cup confectioner's sugar
- Pinch nutmeg
- ¼ teaspoons rum essence

MMMMMMMMMMMMMMMMMMMMMMMMMMM

Methods:

1. Preheat the main oven to 350 degrees F. Grease a 9" springform tin. Set to one side.

2. Combine the baking powder, flour, cinnamon, salt, and nutmeg in a bowl.

3. In a second bowl, beat together the sugar, butter, eggnog, egg, and essences.

4. Add the dry ingredients to the wet a batch at a time and stir until just combined.

5. Pour the batter into the cake tin.

6. Next, make the topping. Combine the sugar, flour, nutmeg, and cinnamon. Rub the butter into the mixture until crumbly. Scatter the mixture over the cake batter and sprinkle over the white chocolate chips.

7. Place in the oven and bake for 40 minutes until golden. Allow to completely cool.

8. In the meantime, make the glaze. Whisk together the eggnog, sugar, nutmeg, and rum essence until combined. Drizzle over the cooled cake.

(30) Boozy Eggnog Crème Brulee

Eggnog just got classier! These boozy crème brulees are a delicious dinner party-worthy dessert.

Yield: 9

Preparation Time: 1hour

List of Ingredients:

- 2 cups heavy whipping cream
- 2 cups readymade eggnog
- ⅓ cup + 3 tablespoons granulated sugar
- Yolks of 8 medium eggs
- 1 teaspoon vanilla essence
- ¼ teaspoons nutmeg
- 2 tablespoons spiced rum
- 3 tablespoons brown sugar

MMMMMMMMMMMMMMMMMMMMMMMMMMM

Methods:

1. Preheat the main oven to 325 degrees F.

2. In a saucepan over moderate heat, whisk together the cream, eggnog, ⅓ cup sugar, and egg yolks. Gently heat until the mixture registers a temperature of 160 degrees F.

3. Take off the heat, stir in the vanilla essence, nutmeg, and rum. Divide the mixture between 10 small ramekins.

4. Arrange the ramekins in a baking pan and pour in 1" of boiling water.

5. Place in the oven and bake for just over 35 minutes.

6. Remove the ramekins from the pan and allow to cool completely. Chill for 5 hours.

7. In a small bowl, combine the remaining 2 tablespoons sugar with the brown sugar. Sprinkle an even amount over the top of each crème brulee. Melt the sugar using a kitchen blowtorch.

8. Serve straight away,

(31) Vanilla Eggnog Cookies

Soft, chewy cookies flavored with spices and eggnog are perfect served with an ice cold glass of milk.

Yield: 24

Preparation Time: 40mins

List of Ingredients:

- 2 teaspoons baking powder
- 2¼ cups all-purpose flour
- ½ teaspoons nutmeg
- ½ teaspoons cinnamon
- ½ cup brown sugar
- ½ cup white sugar
- ¾ cup butter (softened)
- 1 teaspoon vanilla essence
- ½ cup ready-made eggnog
- Yolks of 2 large eggs

MMMMMMMMMMMMMMMMMMMMMMMMMMMM

Methods:

1. Preheat the main oven to 350 degrees F. Grease 2 cookie sheets.

2. Combine the baking powder, flour, nutmeg, and cinnamon in a large bowl.

3. Beat together the sugars and butter until fluffy followed by the vanilla essence, eggnog, and egg yolks.

4. Fold the dry ingredients into the wet until combined.

5. Drop small spoonfuls of the cookie dough onto the cookie sheets and bake in the oven for approximately 12 minutes until golden.

6. Take out of the oven and allow to cool completely before serving.

(32) Celebration Eggnog Trifle

This celebration-worthy, layered trifle combines eggnog and almond pudding, angel food cake, raspberry jam, and a cloud of vanilla whip cream for a texture and flavor sensation.

Yield: 10

Preparation Time: 2hours 20mins

List of Ingredients:

- 1 (3.4 ounce) package instant vanilla pudding
- ¾ cup whole milk (chilled)
- 2 cups readymade eggnog
- ½ teaspoons almond essence
- 1½ cups heavy whipping cream (whipped)
- 1 (10½ ounce) angel food cake (sliced)
- 1 cup raspberry jam
- 2 tablespoons powdered sugar
- ½ teaspoons vanilla essence
- Maraschino cherries

MMMMMMMMMMMMMMMMMMMMMMMMMMMM

Methods:

1. In a bowl, whisk together the vanilla pudding and milk until combined. Add the eggnog and almond essence, stir to combine. Fold in one cup of the whipped cream. Set to one side.

2. Arrange a ¼ of the sliced cake in the base of a large serving bowl. Top with a third of the jam. Spoon over a cup of the eggnog pudding. Repeat these layers twice more.

3. Cover with plastic wrap and chill for a couple of hours.

4. Fold the sugar and vanilla essence into the remaining whip cream and spoon over the trifle. Decorate with maraschino cherries and serve straight away.

(33) Pumpkin Eggnog Pie

Make your pumpkin pie even more festive with a good glug of creamy eggnog.

Yield: 8

Preparation Time: 1hour 10mins

List of Ingredients:

- 1¼ cups eggnog
- 15 ounces canned pumpkin
- 3 medium eggs
- ⅔ cup granulated sugar
- ¼ teaspoons salt
- 1½ teaspoons pumpkin pie spice
- 1 (9") unbaked pie shell

MMMMMMMMMMMMMMMMMMMMMMMMMMM

Methods:

1. Preheat the main oven to 375 degrees F.

2. In a bowl. Combine the eggnog, pumpkin, egg, sugar, salt, and pie spice. Spoon the mixture into the pie shell and bake in the oven for just over an hour until set.

3. Chill until ready to serve.

(34) Cranberry and Eggnog Bread Pudding

Soft and squishy bread pudding with eggnog custard and tangy cranberries is a fun, festive dessert for all the family.

Yield: 9

Preparation Time: 1hour

List of Ingredients:

- 2 cups readymade eggnog
- 4 medium eggs
- ½ cup dried cranberries
- ¾ cup glazed pecans (finely chopped)
- 6 cups soft dinner rolls (cubed)

MMMMMMMMMMMMMMMMMMMMMMMMMMMM

Methods:

1. Preheat the main oven to 375 degrees F. Grease an 8" square baking dish.

2. Whisk together the eggnog and eggs. Fold the cranberries, pecans, and dinner rolls until combined. Set aside for 20 minutes to soften.

3. Transfer the mixture to the baking dish and bake in the oven for just over 35 minutes until golden and puffed. Serve warm.

(35) Holiday Eggnog Mousse

Welcome in the holiday with a dish of creamy eggnog mousse.

Yield: 4

Preparation Time: 45mins

List of Ingredients:

- 2 teaspoons unflavored gelatin
- 2 cups low-fat eggnog
- 2 tablespoons sugar
- ⅛ teaspoons ground cinnamon
- ⅛ teaspoons ground nutmeg
- ½ teaspoons vanilla essence
- 1 cup low-fat whipped topping (divided)
- Ground nutmeg

MMMMMMMMMMMMMMMMMMMMMMMMMMM

Methods:

1. In a pan, scatter the gelatin over the eggnog, and allow to stand for 60 seconds.

2. Over low heat, while stirring, heat until the gelatin entirely dissolves.

3. Stir in the sugar along with the cinnamon and nutmeg until the sugar dissolves.

4. Transfer the mixture to a bowl and place in the fridge until the mixture thickens.

5. Beat the mixture until it's fluffy and light and beat in approximately a ¾ cup of the whipped topping along with the vanilla essence. Divide the dessert between 4 dishes.

6. Transfer the dishes to the fridge, to firm.

7. Top with the remaining whipped topping and garnish with nutmeg.

(36) Eggnog Flan

This classic Latin dessert gets a festive makeover with an irresistible eggnog flavor.

Yield: 6-8

Preparation Time: 9hours 15mins

List of Ingredients:

Caramel:

- 1 teaspoon water
- 1 cup granulated sugar

Flan:

- ¼ cup whole milk
- 1 (14 ounce) can condensed milk
- 5 medium eggs
- ¾ cup eggnog

MMMMMMMMMMMMMMMMMMMMMMMMMMMM

Methods:

1. Preheat the main oven to 350 degrees F.

2. First, prepare the caramel. Combine the water and sugar in a saucepan over moderate heat. Stir occasionally until the sugar comes to a boil.

3. Pour the caramel into a pie plate and allow to cool.

4. Next, prepare the flan. Add the milks, eggs, and eggnogs to a blender and blitz until smooth. Pour the mixture over the cooled caramel. Cover with aluminum foil and arrange in a baking tin. Pour in 1" of boiling water.

5. Place in the oven and cook for 40 minutes.

6. Take out of the oven and completely cool. Chill overnight.

(37) Glazed Eggnog Donuts

These golden donut puffs with sticky-sweet glaze are truly irresistible.

Yield: 8

Preparation Time: 45mins

List of Ingredients:

Donuts:

- 3 tablespoons canola oil
- 1 medium egg
- 6 tablespoons ready-made eggnog
- 1 teaspoon rum essence
- 1 cup all-purpose flour
- 1 teaspoon baking powder
- 3 tablespoons granulated sugar
- ½ teaspoons salt

Glaze:

- 1 cup confectioner's sugar
- 2½ tablespoons readymade eggnog
- ¼ teaspoons rum essence

MMMMMMMMMMMMMMMMMMMMMMMMMMM

Methods:

1. Preheat the main oven to 325 degrees F. Grease a donut pan.

2. Beat together the canola oil, egg, eggnog, and rum essence. Mix in the flour, baking powder, sugar, and salt.

3. Spoon the batter into the donut pan. Bake in the oven for approximately 12 minutes.

4. In the meantime, make the glaze.

5. Stir together the sugar, eggnog, and rum essence. Dip the donuts halfway into the glaze while still warm.

(38) Eggnog and Cranberry Icebox Cake

Classic icebox cake gets an exciting festive twist with store-bought eggnog, fresh berries, and ladyfinger biscuits. It's the perfect crowd-pleasing Christmas treat.

Yield: 12

Preparation Time: 8hours 20mins

List of Ingredients:

- 40 ladyfinger biscuits (split)
- 1 pint cranberry sorbet
- 3 cups store-bought eggnog
- 1 cup evaporated milk
- ½ cup sour cream
- 2 (3.4 ounce) packs instant vanilla pudding mix
- Fresh raspberries
- Fresh mint leaves

MMMMMMMMMMMMMMMMMMMMMMMMMMMMMM

Methods:

1. Arrange 24 ladyfinger biscuits around the edge of an ungreased 9" springform pan.

2. Place the remaining biscuits over the base of the pan.

3. Spoon the sorbet over the biscuits, cover the pan and transfer to the freezer for half an hour.

4. In a mixing bowl, beat the eggnog along with the milk, sour cream and vanilla pudding mix for a couple of minutes until thickened. Spoon the mixture over the sorbet, cover, transfer to the freezer, overnight.

5. When you are ready to serve, take the pan out of the freezer between 5-10 minutes before cutting into slices.

6. Garnish with fresh raspberries and mint.

(39) Gingerbread Eggnog French Toast Bake

This warming French toast bake with rich eggnog and gingerbread spices is a truly delicious way to start the day or end the night.

Yield: 12

Preparation Time: 1hour 10mins

List of Ingredients:

- Nonstick spray

French Toast:

- 12 cups French bread (one day old, cubed)
- 1¾ cup readymade eggnog
- 8 medium eggs
- ¼ cup maple syrup
- ½ cup molasses
- 1 tablespoon vanilla essence
- 1¼ powdered ginger
- 1½ teaspoons cinnamon
- Pinch salt
- ¼ teaspoons cloves

Topping:

- ¼ cup all-purpose flour
- ¼ cup brown sugar
- 1 teaspoon cinnamon
- ¼ teaspoons nutmeg
- ½ teaspoons powdered ginger
- Pinch salt
- Pinch cloves
- ¼ cup butter

Syrup:

- 1½ cups readymade eggnog
- ½ cup maple syrup

MMMMMMMMMMMMMMMMMMMMMMMMMMM

Methods:

1. Preheat the main oven to 350 degrees F. Spritz a 13x9" baking dish with nonstick spray.

2. Add the cubed bread to a large bowl and set to one side.

3. In a second bowl, beat together the eggnog, eggs, maple syrup, molasses, vanilla essence, ginger, cinnamon, salt, and cloves. Pour the mixture over the bread and gently toss to coat.

4. Transfer the mixture to the baking dish.

5. Next, prepare the topping. Combine the flour, sugar, cinnamon, nutmeg, ginger, salt, and cloves. Cut in the butter until crumbly. Sprinkle over the French toast.

6. Place in the oven and bake for an hour until golden and puffy.

7. Take out of the oven and allow to cool for 10 minutes.

8. In the meantime, combine the eggnog and maple syrup in a saucepan over moderate heat. Bring to a simmer and cook until the mixture reduces by half.

9. Serve the syrup with the baked French toast.

(40) Festive Eggnog Fudge

Enjoy a taste of the holidays in every melt-in-the-mouth creamy.

Yield: 32

Preparation Time: 1hour 15mins

List of Ingredients:

- Nonstick cooking spray
- ½ cup butter
- 1⅔ cups sugar
- ¾ cup eggnog
- 2 cups white chocolate chips
- 1 (7 ounce) jar marshmallow crème
- 2¼ teaspoons vanilla essence
- Nutmeg (to garnish)

MMMMMMMMMMMMMMMMMMMMMMMMMMM

Methods:

1. Line an 8" square baking dish with foil and spritz with nonstick cooking spray.

2. In a large pan, over moderate-high heat, combine the butter with the sugar and eggnog and bring to boil, while continually stirring until the temperature registers 234 degrees F.

3. Remove the pan from the heat and stir in the chocolate chips until silky smith.

4. Next, stir in the marshmallow crème along with the vanilla essence, stirring until smooth.

5. Pour the mixture into the prepared baking dish and with a spatula, smooth.

6. Garnish with nutmeg and transfer to the fridge for 60 minutes before cutting into 64 squares.

About the Author

A native of Indianapolis, Indiana, Valeria Ray found her passion for cooking while she was studying English Literature at Oakland City University. She decided to try a cooking course with her friends and the experience changed her forever. She enrolled at the Art Institute of Indiana which offered extensive courses in the culinary Arts. Once Ray dipped her toe in the cooking world, she never looked back.

When Valeria graduated, she worked in French restaurants in the Indianapolis area until she became the head chef at one of the 5-star establishments in the area. Valeria's attention to taste and visual detail caught the eye of a local business person who expressed an interest in publishing her recipes. Valeria began her secondary career authoring cookbooks and e-books which she tackled with as much talent and gusto as her first career. Her passion for food leaps off the page of her books which have colourful anecdotes and stunning pictures of dishes she has prepared herself.

Valeria Ray lives in Indianapolis with her husband of 15 years, Tom, her daughter, Isobel and their loveable Golden Retriever, Goldy. Valeria enjoys cooking special dishes in her large, comfortable kitchen where the family gets involved in preparing meals. This successful, dynamic chef is an inspiration to culinary students and novice cooks everywhere.

Author's Afterthoughts

Thank you for Purchasing my book and taking the time to read it from front to back. I am always grateful when a reader chooses my work and I hope you enjoyed it!

With the vast selection available online, I am touched that you chose to be purchasing my work and take valuable time out of your life to read it. My hope is that you feel you made the right decision.

I very much would like to know what you thought of the book. Please take the time to write an honest and informative review on Amazon.com. Your experience and opinions will be of great benefit to me and those readers looking to make an informed choice.

With much thanks,

Valeria Ray

Printed in Great Britain
by Amazon